# Surrey

### Edited by Michelle Afford

Young**Writers**

First published in Great Britain in 2007 by:
Young Writers
Remus House
Coltsfoot Drive
Peterborough
PE2 9JX
Telephone: 01733 890066
Website: www.youngwriters.co.uk

SB ISBN 978-1 84431 123 1

# Foreword

Young Writers was established in 1991 and has been passionately devoted to the promotion of reading and writing in children and young adults ever since. The quest continues today. Young Writers remains as committed to the nurturing of poetic and literary talent as ever.

This year's Young Writers competition has proven as vibrant and dynamic as ever and we are delighted to present a showcase of the best poetry from across the UK and in some cases overseas. Each poem has been selected from a wealth of *Little Laureates* entries before ultimately being published in this, our sixteenth primary school poetry series.

Once again, we have been supremely impressed by the overall quality of the entries we have received. The imagination, energy and creativity which has gone into each young writer's entry made choosing the poems a challenging and often difficult but ultimately hugely rewarding task - the general high standard of the work submitted ensured this opportunity to bring their poetry to a larger appreciative audience.

We sincerely hope you are pleased with this final collection and that you will enjoy *Little Laureates Surrey* for many years to come.

# Contents

| | |
|---|---:|
| Eleanor Smith  (9) | 75 |
| Timothy Greaves  (10) | 76 |
| Ben Holden  (10) | 77 |
| Divesh Mungur  (10) | 78 |
| Rowan Cole  (10) | 79 |
| Helena Ritter  (10) | 80 |
| Grace Mitchell  (11) | 81 |
| Tom Wainwright  (10) | 82 |
| Charlotte Curran  (10) | 83 |
| Bethany Field  (11) | 84 |
| Elis Tyre  (11) | 85 |
| Emma Sheppard  (10) | 86 |
| Emma Wade  (11) | 87 |
| Darryl Couzens  (10) | 88 |
| Liam Cooke  (11) | 89 |

**Bramley School**
| | |
|---|---:|
| Lily Jones  (9) | 90 |

**Cheam Common Junior School**
| | |
|---|---:|
| Chloe Ivens  (10) | 91 |
| Rachel Smith  (10) | 92 |
| Milana Svaldenyte  (10) | 93 |
| Dinah Mehnaz Ali  (11) | 94 |
| Chloe Wall  (11) | 95 |
| Heather Phillpot  (9) | 96 |
| Elle Gentle  (11) | 97 |
| Joony Han  (10) | 98 |
| Laura El-Bahrawy  (10) | 99 |
| Amba Storm Corsini  (10) | 100 |
| Zibran Ahmed  (9) | 101 |
| Emily Roach  (10) | 102 |
| Leah Dennis  (11) | 103 |
| Georgia Flint  (10) | 104 |
| Jamie Scarborough  (9) | 105 |
| Suzy Astwood  (10) | 106 |
| Elle Sinclair  (11) | 107 |
| Rachel Turner  (10) | 108 |
| Priya Patel  (9) | 109 |
| Ana Popovic  (7) | 110 |
| Ryan Lee Shankar  (8) | 111 |

| | |
|---|---|
| Alexander Sattar  (10) | 147 |
| Antonio Lising  (10) | 148 |
| Jasmin Hayward  (10) | 149 |
| Shannon White  (10) | 150 |
| Bobby Hall  (9) | 151 |
| Tiffany Morant  (10) | 152 |
| Hollie Nixon  (10) | 153 |
| Tyler Pepperell  (10) | 154 |
| Glen Wright  (10) | 155 |
| Ashley Allen  (10) | 156 |
| Maisie Billingham  (10) | 157 |
| Bethany Dunn  (10) | 158 |
| Brandon Johnson  (10) | 159 |
| Shannon Mills  (11) | 160 |
| Arjunn Senthilnathan  (11) | 161 |
| Jonathan Williamson-Taylor  (10) | 162 |
| Ellie Hale  (10) | 163 |

## Green Wrythe Primary School

| | |
|---|---|
| George Kenton | 164 |
| Mitchell Murdoch  (7) | 165 |
| Ben Honey | 166 |
| Joshua Garrod  (8) | 167 |
| Charli Barrie  (8) | 168 |
| Florence Harris | 169 |
| Amy Fountain  (7) | 170 |
| Chelsie Gumble | 171 |
| Ellie Colvin  (9) | 172 |
| Laura Allen  (7) | 173 |
| Rhys Smith  (9) | 174 |
| Daisy Hunt  (7) | 175 |
| Bradd Healy  (9) | 176 |
| Katie Davis-Sullivan  (8) | 177 |
| Hayden Berriedale-Pocock  (9) | 178 |
| Billie-Jo Morgan  (8) | 179 |
| Rachel O'Neill  (9) | 180 |
| Caitlin Logue  (8) | 181 |
| Evan Hewes  (9) | 182 |
| Charlotte Gant  (7) | 183 |
| Paige Waller  (7) | 184 |
| Charlie-Jade Mills  (9) | 185 |

# The Poems

# My Furry Friend

M e and
Y ou

F luffy pony,
U nbelievably cute,
R eally soft and cuddly,
R eady for absolutely anything,
Y ou are my favourite of them all.

F riends at the day's end,
R arely without a smile,
I ncredibly intelligent,
E xcitingly unusual,
N ever lets you down,
D arling Spotty.

**Ellie Clancy  (8)**
**All Saints CE Primary School**

# People Around The World

There are a lot of people around the world
with different coloured skin.
White, black, brown, yellow,
with different types of languages.
But God loves us all the same.

**Lizzie Martin  (8)**
**All Saints CE Primary School**

# Love

Love, love in the air,
Floating around everywhere,
In the sky but you can't see,
There is enough love for you and me.
Sharing love here and there,
There will be enough to share,
And if you feel you're not being loved,
Hey, wait until the next Valentine's Day!

**Reni Animashaun  (10)**
**All Saints CE Primary School**

# What You See On A Farm From A Railway Carriage

*(Inspired by 'From a Railway Carriage' by Robert Louis Stevenson)*

We see fields and meadows of sheep and cattle.
We see men riding horses and mounting their saddles.
We see ducks in the pond and pigs at the fence,
And farmer taking a break on the bench.

We see sheep in the barn and the cows are all out,
Grazing and grazing and mucking about.
We see birds in the trees and twigs on the ground,
And dogs chasing cats round and around.

We see haystacks and haystacks on fields full of crops.
We see chickens and hens being watched by a fox.
We see a man in a car with nowt to park it.
We see a cart full of eggs all ready for market.

**Harry Brodie  (10)**
**All Saints CE Primary School**

# Nature

All nature is so pretty,
All colourful and bright,
Tulips and buttercups,
And daffodils in light.

All nature is so pretty,
A great big willow tree,
Or may be an oak tree,
It doesn't matter much to me.

All nature is so pretty,
The flowers and the trees,
They look lovely all year round,
So that makes me happy!

**Ruth Davison  (10)**
**All Saints CE Primary School**

# Matchstick

Matchstick girls and matchstick boys
Matchstick house, matchstick toys
Matchstick men and matchstick hats
Matchstick dogs and matchstick cats
Matchstick women in matchstick coats
Matchstick rivers, matchstick boats
Matchstick hands, matchstick beds
Matchstick houses, matchstick prams
Matchstick factories, matchstick trams
Matchstick flowers, matchstick trees
Matchstick fields, matchstick bees
Matchstick grass and matchstick flies
Matchstick pounds, matchstick butterflies
Matchstick clouds, matchstick grounds
Matchstick sounds, matchstick hounds.

**Elliesha Sadler (10)**
**All Saints CE Primary School**

# A Journey Through My Body

A journey through my body
The brain is where I'll start,
I'll see my blood and organs
And go through every part.

The brain is like a big blancmange
Sitting on a stalk,
It helps you think, move, read and write
It even helps you talk!

Off to the lungs, here we go,
The air goes in and out,
It brings oxygen in
And helps us to scream and shout!

*Boom, boom, boom, boom,*
The pounding of my heart,
Pumping blood around my body,
It plays an important part!

This is my stomach
Where my food goes,
I digest it in here
And it smells like my toes!

*Ssssssshhhhhh,*
What's that? It's time to go
Through my bladder
And off I go!

**Anna Everest  (10)**
**All Saints CE Primary School**

# Bedtime

B edtime is a time to go to sleep,
E very evening my sleep is quite deep,
D one for the day and I need a nap,
T omorrow I might wear my football cap.
I   have to go to bed at nine,
M y mum sits downstairs drinking wine.
E nd of time to get to sleep,

Extra time in bed though I'd like to keep.

**Cameron Starr  (10)**
**All Saints CE Primary School**

# What Am I?

My body
parts are round.
I sit there on the
ground.
I stand out there
all week,
where it is
always bleak

**Ben Whittaker  (10)**
**All Saints CE Primary School**

# Mr F Finger

Nice and crumbly,
Very yummy.
Soft centre,
Fills my tummy.
Made of fish,
Perfect dish.
Golden brown,
Comes to town.

**Jonathan Fahy  (10)**
**All Saints CE Primary School**

# The Problem With Snow

The problem with snow,
Is that it glows.
In the dark,
It makes the dogs bar.
You can play in it,
But it is a bit slishy and slushy.
It makes you feel funny.
If you run,
It'll trip you in fun.
When you hit, *smack!*
It goes down your back.
If it melts,
You'll find your belt,
But the fun and the sculptures
Will disappear like vultures
And you'll have to wait till next year.

**Charlie Constable  (10)**
**All Saints CE Primary School**

# Snowman!

Snowman cold
Snowman funny.

Snowman with a big, round tummy!
Snow man melts in the sun.
He is gone in front of everyone!

**Yasmin Hawa  (10)**
**All Saints CE Primary School**

# Little Red Riding Hood

There was a young girl who strolled through the wood,
With her little red cape and her little red hood.
On her way she got a surprise,
Her mum had told her to think and be wise.
Little Red Riding Hood did what she said,
She ignored some noises, put them out of her head.

A wolf knocked on Grandma's door,
Wolfie pinned her to the floor.
He gobbled her up in one big bite,
Then he went inside and turned on the light.
He put on some clothes and climbed into bed,
Then he curled all his hairs on his colossal head.
*Knock,, knock, knock,* there was a bang below,
Wolfie cried, 'Hello, hello!'
Little Red Riding Hood crept up the stairs,
She entered the room spotting a trail of hairs.

'What big teeth you've got.'
'I know, I know, there's quite a lot.'
Suddenly Wolfie leapt out of bed,
Not bothering if he bumped his head.
He pounced on Little Red Riding Hood,
But just then, before he could,
She jumped and kicked him really hard,
He flew out the window and across the yard.
Wolfie went down and down and landed with a *thump,*
Then Grandma came flying out and fell with a *bump*.
Little Red Riding Hood ran as fast as she could,
In her little red cape and her little red hood.
Grandma was put in hospital,
Wearing a furry wolf-skin shawl.
Mr Wolf was put up for sale,
But Little Red Riding Hood lived to tell the tale.

**Andrianna Martin  (10)**
**All Saints CE Primary School**

## Off To Bed

'Time for bed,' shouted Mum
so I fled to my bed
and rested my head
upon my velvet pillow
and I floated off
to sleep.

**Jacob Trappitt  (11)**
**All Saints CE Primary School**

# Missing You

I miss you and I wish you were here
Where are you my darling dear?
I weep and weep and get no sleep
This pain inside me feels so deep
I wish that you had never died
I wish to be right by your side.

**Afia Dapaah-Danquah  (11)**
**All Saints CE Primary School**

# Big Beach

B ig beach is the best beach in the world
I surfed on the waves
G oing *splish, splash, splosh!*

B athing in the sun
E ating delicious Cornettos
A ll the people have lots of fun
C ooling in the shade of umbrellas
H oping this day will never end.

**Emma Norman (7)**
**All Saints CE Primary School**

# The Final Battle Of A Celtic Warrior

I see in my body that I'm freaked out
from the spears coming out of the air.
I hear the air swords swooshing like a plane crashing.
I feel like I'm stabbed in the heart
and my veins are popping spitting blood out.
I smell flaming burnt houses and wood crushing me.
I touch a silver sword, slitting the Romans' throats.

**Joshua Long  (9)**
**Beacon Hill Primary School**

# The Magic Box

*(Based on 'Magic Box' by Kit Wright)*

I will put in my box . . .
Bananas bouncing on a ball with a bully boy.
A jumping John jumping joyfully through the jungle.
And a sinking ship swishing to shore.

I will put in my box . . .
A crab scuttling sideways towards my face.
A duck saying *ribbit* and a frog going *quack*.
And a burglar hugging a little girl.

I will put in my box . . .
A lilac secret whispered quietly in my ear.
A happy smile from playing on my trampoline.
And a sad face from when my rabbit ran away.

My box is designed in soft gold linen
With a silver moon looking curious,
And rules at the top,
With sand and shells on the side.

In my box I will fly up to the moon and travel through time,
To see who I will be . . .
Who will I be I wonder.

**Abby Ray (8)**
**Beacon Hill Primary School**

# My Magic Box

*(Based on 'Magic Box' by Kit Wright)*

I will put in the box . . .
A dancing dolphin doing dances
A breath of flame from a fierce fat monster,
A sizzling sausage swimming in the supper pan.

I will put in the box . . .
The sweet smell of lavender
A taste of sugar fresh from the sugar cane
The sound of soft sea hitting a rock.

I will put in the box . . .
The happy and sad people
The good and bad animals
And the 25th hour of the day.

I will put in the box . . .
The 13th month
A submarine on dry land
And a car underwater.

My box is fashioned from chocolate
Gold and amethyst with crystals on the sides
And ribbons on top.

I shall swim in my box
With a great blue whale
And fall onto a silver star
The colour of mist.

**Lauren Caffrey (8)**
**Beacon Hill Primary School**

# The Magic Box

*(Based on 'Magic Box' by Kit Wright)*

I will put in my box . . .
A crispy cookie crumbling slowly because it is sloppy
And crumbling like soft tea and smelling like hot chocolate
And feeling like smooth skin.

I will put in my box . . .
A little fluffy bunny
Eating a huge carrot
And a cup of tea.

I will put in my box . . .
The darkest day
And the brightest night
When you are all asleep.

My box is made out of . . .
Shiny metal and silver
And smells like perfume made from lavender.

In my box I will . . .
Fly to Africa to see the country
And see other animals
And play with the elephants.

**Livvi Maynard  (8)**
**Beacon Hill Primary School**

# My Magic Box

*(Based on 'Magic Box' by Kit Wright)*

I will put in my box . . .
The gum of a gooey guzzle monster
And the murder of the skull snake,
The slime of sloppiness, slide side to side.

I will put in my box . . .
A packet of chips with tomato sauce on,
A sip of white non-salted sea
And a wave splashing high.

I will put in my box . . .
Kindness, green like the blazing grass
And my ancient great, great, great grandpa
And a newborn baby's first word.

I will put in my box . . .
900,000 days in a year, 4000,000 Santa visits,
A man barking
And a dog speaking.

My box is full of sports cars
Racing to the humans,
Its hinges are made out of crisps.

I shall race in my box,
On the street, winning races,
Then win lots of money by betting,
Then I'll be rich.

**Jonathan Worman  (9)**
**Beacon Hill Primary School**

# Darkness

Darkness is black like the skin of a spooky panther,
It sounds like dark mushy medicine bubbling towards me,
It tastes like cold blood malfunctioning into burnt bits of coal,
It smells like the inside of someone's organ pipe,
It looks like the inside of someone's dumb brain,
It feels like a tiger pouncing onto the inside of my belly,
It reminds me of hundreds of deaths every day.

**Edward Garrett (8)**
**Beacon Hill Primary School**

# The Magic Box

*(Based on 'Magic Box' by Kit Wright)*

I will put in my box . . .
A chocolate cookie crumbled by a chicken.

I will put in my box . . .
A star shining in the sky.

I will put in my box . . .
An old piece of cheese that is one hundred years old.

I will put in my box . . .
An eighth day of the week,
A cat that barks woof,
And a dog that purrs miaow.

My box is made from . . .
Ice and stones and gold with crystals on it,
The hinges are the hind leg bones of a frog.

I shall play rugby in my box
At the biggest stadium ever,
With my box I will score the winning try for England.

**Edward Vass (8)**
**Beacon Hill Primary School**

# The Magic Box

*(Based on 'Magic Box' by Kit Wright)*

I will put in my box . . .
The flash of a fabulous fish,
Water from the spout of a Pacific whale,
South Siamese snakes eating.

I will put in the box . . .
A shark with a sniffing nose,
A chomp of the finest chocolate chip cookie,
A sparkling flash from a leaping firework.

I will put in my box . . .
Golden gravity spinning around the Earth,
The last breath from Tutankamen's mouth,
And the first word from the lips of a baby.

I will put in my box . . .
A 13th month and a purple river,
A Chelsea footballer in a smart car,
And a doctor in a Porsche.

My box is built from chocolate, silver and gold,
With moons on the top and my autograph in the corners,
Its hinges are the jaws of a lion.

I will drive in my box
From the cold, British beaches
To the pizza-loving beaches of Italy,
Whose colour is that of the brightest giraffe.

**Alex Chubb  (8)**
**Beacon Hill Primary School**

# Hate

Hate is black like a deep, dark hole.
Hate sounds like a lion roaring.
Hate tastes like a sour lemon in your mouth.
Hate smells like a hot, burning pepper.
Hate looks like a tiger looking for his prey.
Hate feels like your heart getting broken.
Hate reminds me of breaking up with my friend.

**Jack Jefferies (8)**
**Beacon Hill Primary School**

# Magic Box

*(Based on 'Magic Box' by Kit Wright)*

I will put in the box . . .
The strange sounding song of a singing sailor,
Water lilies from the nearby pond,
The weird, wacky cackle from a witch.

I will put in the box . . .
A strange statue from a museum, still smiling,
The tip of a terrifying pteradactyl,
The smell of an old, smelly lump of cheese.

I will put in the box . . .
Five indigo rules, not to be broken,
The happiness of laughing,
The sadness of saying goodbye.

I will put in the box . . .
An eleventh side of a decagon,
A showjumper in a tree,
And a monkey on a show horse.

My box is designed with silk from the Queen's curtains,
It has a gold lock and keyhole,
And whispers and silence cover the sides.

I will take my box . . .
Through imaginary worlds with fantasy, dragons and unicorns,
And rainbows leading to a pot of gold.

**Alexia Kaloudis (9)**
**Beacon Hill Primary School**

# The Magic Box

*(Based on 'Magic Box' by Kit Wright)*

I will put in my box . . .
A blow of the windy white wind through the window.
Pigs pushing pathetic pigeons.
Dolphins drinking dodgy drinks.

I will put in my box . . .
A sip of milk from the coolest coconut.
A scoop of cocoa beans fresh from the plant.
Sweet smelling perfumes from the best people.

I will put in my box . . .
Three golden wishes.
The last leaf of an oak tree.
The first shine of a new moon.

I will put in my box . . .
A newborn adult.
A mouse chasing a cat.
A dog walking his man.

My box is fashioned from gold and diamonds.
It's bigger on the inside than out.
Its hinges are made of golden silk.

I shall play in my box
In a great big tree camp which turns
Into a shuttle ship transporting
Me through time and space and
Different galaxies.

**Jamie Madgwick  (9)**
**Beacon Hill Primary School**

# The Magic Box

*(Based on 'Magic Box' by Kit Wright)*

I will put in the box . . .
The smell of a sour, savoury salad sandwich,
Smoke from the fire of a fierce dragon,
A satisfied, sorry, slimy snake.

I will put in the box . . .
A pretty flower with a rumbling stalk,
The smell of a brand new fragrance in the bathroom,
The look of an endangered tiger snoring in his sleep.

I will put in the box . . .
Two tiny silver hugs,
The loud voice of an old uncle,
The quiet cry of a young baby.

I will put in my box . . .
A 14 month and an ancient child,
A dog that miaows,
And a cat that barks.

My box is created from chewing gum,
Paper and mashed potatoes,
With footballs on the lid
And created dreams on the side.

I shall swim in my box,
In the deep blue, wild Atlantic Ocean,
With all the bright multicoloured tropical fish.

**Pippa Tilney  (9)**
**Beacon Hill Primary School**

# Fear

Fear is green like a slithering snake chasing its prey.
It sounds like a fierce tiger roaring.
It tastes like the terrifying flavour of liquorice.
It smells like ooey-gooey car fumes, grey and dark.
Fear looks like the tooth of a lion digging into its prey.
It feels like a cheetah sprinting at you as if you were dinner.
Fear reminds me of the first time I went to a zoo and I saw a shark.

**Helena Laws (9)**
**Beacon Hill Primary School**

# The Final Battle Of A Celtic Warrior

I can see Celts getting stabbed with poisoned swords,
                                    spears and daggers.
Romans smashing out breath, they have blood dripping down their
                                    vicious faces.

I can hear blazing voices streaming through my head.
Flames bashing my brain telling me not go near the Roman captain.

I can feel blood bursting through my brain.
My heart beating like it's going to burst open.
I feel Romans chopping men into the sand.

The smell is revolting, of Romans.
The breeze of trees, plants and poppies.
Flesh from Roman skulls and our bodies as well.

I can touch the blade on my spear and shield,
About to stab a terrible Roman.
We're all trying to rip the life out of each other.

**Harry Lacey (9)**
**Beacon Hill Primary School**

# Football

F antastic boots for scoring goals
O ur family support Tottenham
O ccupied with winning the game
T uck away a goal
B oots are sometimes magic
A way games are really cruel
L ads working as a team
L ove it, play it!

**Dillon Elrick (9)**
**Beacon Hill Primary School**

# Love

Love is red like a sweet, rosy cherry.
It sounds like a beautiful little bird singing happily.
It tastes like lips crushing together.
It smells like dark, sugary chocolate.
It looks like white, shiny, glittery ducks' eggs.
It feels like a monkey's smooth, glittery, silky fur.
It reminds me of loving other precious people.

**Erika Lorimer  (9)**
**Beacon Hill Primary School**

# My Magic Box

*(Based on 'Magic Box' by Kit Wright)*

I will put in my box . . .
The sound of a snake slithering silently,
Ice drops melting in the sun,
Little mangy mice mooing mysteriously.

I will put in my box . . .
The taste of bitter red wine,
The feel of fire melting my hand,
The sight of a dragon with its flaming red eyes.

I will put in my box . . .
One yellow sound of a newborn baby,
The last word of a sunken ship,
The first body of a floating man.

I will put in my box . . .
Thirty-two days in a never-ending month,
A moon shining brightly,
The sun as dark as a skull.

My box is shiny like stars surrounding the moon,
It has a gleaming gold lid and special silver corners,
The bottom of it has wheels, it teleports me to places,
Its hinges are made of gold and steel plate.

I shall play in my box with all the animals I have,
I shall visit a safari and the moon,
Then I will float around the world,
In a bubble.

**Charlie Newman (8)**
**Beacon Hill Primary School**

# My Magic Box

*(Based on 'Magic Box' by Kit Wright)*

I will put in my box . . .
A shiny silver star sparkling in the sky
A cute cuddly kitten called Kit
And a relaxed foal that will lie down.

I will put in my box . . .
A half horse/dog
With the head of a cat
I will put in my box a cloud that is yellow.

I will put in my box . . .
Pieces of cheese that are one hundred years old
An old piece of bread that has been in my house for ten years
An old haunted castle in the distance.

My box is made out of
Rusty old metal like a box of treasure
Lined with creaking wood
That is very black.

**Hattie Pringle  (8)**
**Beacon Hill Primary School**

# Ghost

G liding silently in the night.
H ooting in the woods coming from an owl.
O ur brains thinking *run away!*
S ausages screaming sourly.
T oddlers playing, not knowing what's coming.

**William Edwards (8)**
**Beacon Hill Primary School**

# My Hate

The colour is red like some burning, hot lava
It sounds like blood dripping down in the distance
It tastes like flaming smoke from chilli peppers
It smells like some mice tails all gathered in a group
It looks like blood all around me.

**Lucy Johnson  (9)**
**Beacon Hill Primary School**

# Grace's Poem

Animal skin isn't pretty,
In fact it is quite a pity,
Why do people do these things?
Maybe it's just to big up their bling.
They use it in fashion shows,
They think it kinda makes them glow.
Well look, I don't agree with this,
In fact I think it's really thick.
If I ever meet the peeps
That kill these poor things
I would pull and heave
And wind them up,
Until they were thin strings.

**Grace Taylor  (9)**
**Beulah Junior School**

# Lion - Haiku

Lion, big and scary.
Hunts through the long grass for food.
Pounces on his food.

**Stephen Pickett  (9)**
**Beulah Junior School**

# My Name's Kiane

My name's Kiane
And I have a friend Diane.
When we get a chance
We both love to dance.
One foot forward, one foot back.
Both hands in the air
*Clap! Clap! Clap!*

When it's all over
People start to cheer,
I say to Diane
*'Hear! Hear! Hear!'*

**Kiane Ashman-Swaby  (10)**
**Beulah Junior School**

# Simply Me

My name's Krishna and I like to swim,
But only because I want to win.
My favourite number is 51,
And I like the red-hot sun.
I also like a little dog,
But not a day of fog.
My best friends are always there,
So I never leave but always care.

I like lots of yummy sweets, then to play a game,
But my sister always cheats.
I like the colour gold,
And a ball that's always rolled.
And I also have a bunny
Who is very funny.
I like the subject maths,
Because you find out lots of facts.

**Krishna Mithani  (10)**
**Beulah Junior School**

# My Name Is Reece

My name is Reece,
I am a great beast,
I love to rhyme,
All the time.

My name is Reece,
I like my sister,
I think she's disgusting
Because she picked her blister.

My name is Reece,
I love to read books,
It's not my hobby,
Although I have an MP3 it gets stuck on hooks.

**Reece Lewis  (10)**
**Beulah Junior School**

# Girls Vs Boys

My name is Shukriya and I love school!
I work hard but I don't play pool
And this is my wonderful rule . . .
Everybody should be smart and learn lots of art,
Learn a lot and win a jackpot!

So all you boys out there, look around,
There are girls everywhere!
'Cause we are the best, better than the rest,
Also in east or west!
What do you think?
Yes or no?

**Shukriya Niazi (9)**
**Beulah Junior School**

# Haikus

*Meerkat*

The meerkat is small
The meerkat is swift and cool
The meerkat is fast.

*Monkey*

The monkey is strong
The monkey likes to swing fast
The monkey is cool.

*Tiger*

I do like tigers
The big stripes are nice and cool
The tiger is fast.

*Turtle*

Turtle, so, so slow
Turtle shell is hard as rock
Vicious as a cat.

**Sherlock Kaddu & Haydon Bancroft (10)**
Beulah Junior School

# True Or False

Good, true friends are like jewels
Precious and rare
False friends are like leaves
Found anywhere.
So is you friend true?
Is she the person with a heart,
That is careful
Not to tear yours apart?
Or is she false,
Greediness never-ending?
She has a heart
But doesn't care when yours needs mending
Well I guess you will know
When you have a glow
Deep inside
That thing you have been waiting to find.
Well, I have good friends
As you know
I would never leave their side
Even if they go.

**Samantha Ugwuanya  (9)**
**Beulah Junior School**

# How Am I?

My name is Lucrece,
And I like eating crisps,
When people are sad,
I try not to make them feel bad.

When people are cheeky,
I'm not really happy.
I like being friendly,
When people do things kindly.

**Lucrece Wasolua Kibeti  (10)**
**Beulah Junior School**

# My Rap

My name is Shybah,
And I like to play,
I go to sleep late,
But that's OK.
My best friends are Krishna, Hayley and Natasha,
We like to play on the monkey bars together.

I like to watch TV all day long,
My favourite programme is 'The Suite Life of Zack and Cody'
with Brenda Song.

If you want to have fun,
I'm the one.
Now I've finished,
My rap is done.

**Shybah Yunis  (9)**
**Beulah Junior School**

# London

Come to London and see the history.
Go down Bakers Lane
		And see who's to blame for the Great Fire in 1666.
Or go and see where Elizabeth was captured and set free to be Queen.
Even come to see almost everywhere in London
On the Eye see Big Ben and much, much more.

**Heather McSorley  (8)**
**Brambletye Junior School**

# Step Forward

Step forward
To see my world . . .

You will find an emerald sun,
Scorching chocolate cake.

Step forward to see my world . . .

You will find amethyst cliffs,
Gazing down on pearl seas.

Step forward
To see my world . . .

You will find golden flowers,
That smell like fresh cherries.

Step forward
To see my world . . .

You will find topaz tropical trees,
With glowing ruby leaves.

Step forward
To see my world . . .

You will find crystal dragons
Flying through garnet skies.

Step forward
To see my world . . .

You will find sapphire clouds,
Floating in the dazzling skies.

**Chloe Lea  (9)**
**Brambletye Junior School**

# Roses In Heaven

Roses are growing in Heaven,
Daisies are growing there too,
But it takes a place like Heaven
To grow a rose like you.

**Brittany Edge & Jodie Spencer  (9)**
**Brambletye Junior School**

# The Moon

The moon is always up in the sky,
Shining bright like my little light.

The moon looks like a big toenail in the sky,
Kicking the stars until they fly.

The moon is always looking down on the Earth,
Like God is looking down on you.

The moon looks like it is smiling at you,
To make you happy.

**Vicky Holden  (11)**
**Brambletye Junior School**

# The Moon

The moon is like a shiny light
In the darkness of the night.
The moon is like a gold medal
Swinging in the clouds above.

The moon is like
Glitter in the starry sky.
The moon is like a night light
That has been switched on.

The moon is like a child asleep,
When the child wakes up
The moon moves along.

**Aleema Baux  (10)**
**Brambletye Junior School**

# The Moon

The moon is like a crystal banana
Just sitting in the sky.
The moon is like a football
Floating in the sky.
The moon is like a TV
Watching all of you sleep.
The moon is like a ghost
Making all of the stars shine.
The moon is like a song
Singing all of you to sleep.
The moon is like a mum
Waking up all the stars.
The moon is like a bright, shiny light
That haunts the night.

**Amee Brunt  (10)**
**Brambletye Junior School**

# The River

The river is a small boy
Rocking in his chair,
Swinging and singing
To the river.

The river is a dancer
Dancing to the breeze,
Showing off her amazing
New acrobatic trick.

The river is a rock star
Rocking to the loud waves,
Showing his skills
To all the little children.

**Rachael Emmerson (11)**
**Brambletye Junior School**

# The River

The river is a race car driver
Speeding over the ground.

The river is a speedboat driver
Splashing through the sea.

The river is an athlete
Jumping really high, warming up to run.

The river is a boy
Walking in a crowd, jumping over people.

The river is a young person
Jumping out of his house.

**Noaman Iqbal (10)**
**Brambletye Junior School**

# The Moon

The moon is like a shiny globe
That is making the sun fade away
The moon is like a ghost waking up
And making the sky go dark
The moon is like a shiny, white circle
That does not turn around

The moon is like a shiny light
It makes me feel bright
The moon is a snowman
That glows in the dark
The moon is a white paper
It's gentle, soft and calm

The moon is like a bright window
That has only just been bought
The moon is like rain dripping down
It never stops, it carries on
The moon is like a baby
It is soft and cuddly.

**Taiye Musa  (10)**
**Brambletye Junior School**

# Moon

The moon is like a night dragon
It lights up the sky with fire.

The moon is like a ball of light
That lights the sky with a gaslight of fire.

The moon is like an old man
Lit up and he's really drowsy.

The moon is like a strolling kid in the sky
That glows so bright that it lights the whole night sky.

The moon is a young lady
Who fills the night sky with joy.

**Connor Manning (10)**
**Brambletye Junior School**

# The Moon

The moon is like a shining like a star,
Bright and white and shining at night.
The moon is like a little baby,
Asleep in bed, very cosy, very quiet.

And when the night turns to day,
The baby wakes and the moon goes away,
When the day turns to night,
The baby falls asleep,
The moon comes out,

Just like clouds that come and go,
The moon waxes and wanes all on its own.

**Jade Parsons  (11)**
**Brambletye Junior School**

# Darkness

Darkness is a lost soul, a never-ending black hole
Darkness smells like rotting flesh
Darkness tastes bitter and sour
Darkness sounds like burning pain
Darkness is a searing flame
Darkness feels like an aching boil
Darkness looks like a sharp cook's knife.

**John-Joe Sangster  (10)**
**Brambletye Junior School**

# Fear

Fear tastes like pitch-black sheets.
Fear feels like hot, bubbling lava.
Fear smells like tears and loneliness.
Fear sounds like loud thunder and lightning.
Fear looks like dark grey, gloomy clouds.

What does fear feel like for you?
Fear reminds me of darkness.

**Oliver Holmes (7)**
**Brambletye Junior School**

# Fun

My idea of fun is a big disco
With me controlling the lights
And the different effects dancing round the room.
Fun is the slider of the lights
Make me feel brilliant.
Fun is hearing music bouncing off the wall like a ball.

It smells like food cooking
And tastes like prawn cocktail crisps.
Reminds me of my birthday.

**Christopher Hobbs (7)**
**Brambletye Junior School**

# Laughter

Laughter feels like a surprise.
Laughter sounds like a volcano.
Laughter looks like a roaring dinosaur.
Laughter tastes like eating marshmallows.
Laughter reminds me of laughing.

**Isabelle Wright  (7)**
**Brambletye Junior School**

# Hunger

Hunger tastes like chocolate cake.
Hunger gives you a stomach ache.
Hunger sounds like a rumbly tummy.
Hunger feels like you have got an empty tummy.
Hunger smells like Christmas cake.
Hunger reminds me of food.

**Hannah Curry (7)**
**Brambletye Junior School**

# Sadness

S adness feels like . . .
A hurt kind of feeling inside.
D on't try to remember the thing that's going on.
N ever,
E ver.
S adness looks pitch-black and tastes plain.
S adness sounds dull and smells stinky.

What does sadness remind you of?

**Simran Bahra (8)**
**Brambletye Junior School**

# Anger

Anger feels like horridness.
Anger tastes like fire.
Anger smells like steam.
Anger sounds like a rumble of thunder.
Anger looks really mean.
Anger reminds me of envy.
What does anger remind you of?

**Nathan Barlow  (8)**
**Brambletye Junior School**

# Laughter

Laughter feels like the happy times and fun times of the day.
Laughter tastes like fluffy, soft candyfloss that melts away.
Laughter smells like sweet sugar in sweets.
Laughter sounds like the wind gliding.
Laughter looks like a glittering sun.

Laughter reminds me of things that I have done.
What does laughter remind you of?

**Lily Peters  (7)**
**Brambletye Junior School**

# Fun

Fun tastes like chocolate cake.
Fun feels like having a good time.
Fun sounds really loud!
Fun looks like happiness.
Fun smells like bubbling crisps.
Fun reminds me of playing with my brother and sister
And all my friends.

**Amy McWilliams (8)**
**Brambletye Junior School**

# Hunger

It tastes like lumpy porridge.
It feels like a prickly hedgehog.
It sounds like a monster moaning.
It smells like food slowly getting further away.
It looks like someone in pain.
It reminds me of when I'm ill.

**Beth Hardy  (9)**
**Brambletye Junior School**

# Laughter I Like . . .

It sounds like runners running, like people chattering.
It feels like feathers tickling you, like fairy dust falling on you.
It tastes like someone tickling the back of your throat, like breadcrumbs.
It smells like teddies that have just been washed,
                        like freshly baked bread.
It looks like almost invisible pixies, like gravel rolling.
It reminds me of being on the beach,
Reminds me of running on grass barefoot.

**Charlie Oubridge  (8)**
**Brambletye Junior School**

# Darkness

It smells like toast burning madly.
It looks like black ink spreading over the page.
It tastes like disaster taking over the world.
It sounds like a wave crashing against the rocks.
It feels like rough carpet rubbing against my hand.
It reminds me of a dragon taking over the skies.
Darkness!

**Emily Edwards  (9)**
**Brambletye Junior School**

# Hunger

H unger sounds like someone dying.
H U nger tastes like boring nothingness.
Hu N ger feels like throwing up.
Hun G er smells like mouldy pizza.
Hung E r looks like a baby crawling on the floor.
Hunge R reminds me of a painful adult crawling about.

**Jack Dale (9)**
**Brambletye Junior School**

# Laughter

Laughter feels like elastic bands
Twanging all inside you
And the bubbling of stew
It smells like flowers
Smiling through the hours
It tastes like candy
All sugar-grain sandy
It bursts like popcorn going *bang!*
And big drums going *boom and bam!*
It looks like bubbles going pop
Because it suddenly stops.

It reminds me of excitement!

**Heather Seldon  (9)**
**Brambletye Junior School**

# Darkness

It looks like a black dragon looming over me.
It smells like rotten eggs.
It sounds like children crying.
It tastes of burnt toast.
It reminds me of a big black cave.
It feels like rough carpet.

Darkness.

**Siân Woodfield  (9)**
**Brambletye Junior School**

# Fun With Motorbikes

Rev it up and feel the super speed
Zoom along the track and joy will take over
The jump looms up like Hell's calling
In the back of your mind you hear the crowd going crazy
With sweat dripping down your face and the smell of petrol
You feel horrible
Especially when a deadly turn comes into view
As your face is about to burst
You hear ear-splitting screams.

Rev it up and feel the speed
It's really fun, believe me, I know
Dusty tracks but then, who cares?
The golden cup makes you dare
You hear other bikes but yours is best
You are king, it's so fun
The line is in sight
You cross it first
You've won, you've won
Believe it or not
You really are king
It's great!
The golden cup is *yours!*

**Brandon Harrington-Smith  (9)**
Brambletye Junior School

# The Room Of Doom

I walked through the door into a dark, dark place
Nowhere in the place was the scent of grace
I saw nothing, nothing but a dark, murky door
The place was full of rats scurrying across the floor
That was all I heard, it's all as it is
The place must be the temple of darkness
I could taste cold, murky air
I felt a ball of dust here and there
The smell was nothing but a bit of dust
Getting trapped in my nose
The only place it reminded me of is
The dark, cold night when I could hear footsteps tapping gently
The door opening to reveal green light
Then teleporting to this dark, dark place
All I wanted was to lie in my warm, cosy bed
Not to be in a dark, dusty place
But I found out my time was over there in the dark, freezing place
The green light came again and the scent of grace
And at last I was back in my warm, so cosy bed
Never again shall I go to the place of *dread!*

**Shion Donnison  (9)**
**Brambletye Junior School**

# Opposites

Silence sounds like nothing moving.
Silence tastes like an empty plate.
Silence looks like still bodies.
Silence feels like you haven't got a mate.
Silence smells like frozen ice.
Silence makes you think that you're lonely.

Noise sounds like life and action.
Noise tastes like a great feast.
Noise looks like competitions and races.
Noise feels like there's a great big beast.
Noise smells like hot bubbling water.
Noise makes you think you're having fun!

**Eleanor Smith  (9)**
**Brambletye Junior School**

# Silence

Silence feels like an aching pain
Silence tastes like sour grain
Silence sounds like a constant scream
Silence reminds me of a bad dream
Silence smells like an empty fridge
Silence looks like a broken bridge
Silence feels like a sharp blade
Silence reminds me of a gusty glade.

**Timothy Greaves  (10)**
**Brambletye Junior School**

# Amazing Laughter

Laughter tastes like a drop of sweet strawberry sauce,
Laughter smells like a beautiful summer morning,
Laughter sounds like the song of the singing lark,
Laughter looks like a finished test,
Laughter feels like a cushy couch,
Laughter reminds me of when you win a race.

**Ben Holden  (10)**
**Brambletye Junior School**

# Darkness

Darkness shines like the sun
Darkness smells like Cloud 9
Darkness hugs you like a teddy bear!
I hear the darkness as a joyous hubbub
Darkness tastes like heaven
Darkness makes me feel romantic
Darkness turns my frown upside down!
Darkness is like zero gravity
Darkness reminds me of vomit
Then I hear a continuous *boom*
But it doesn't come towards me, it goes away
It goes down, the darkness, as I stay.

**Divesh Mungur  (10)**
**Brambletye Junior School**

# Darkness

Darkness is a hungry serpent,
that lurks in every house.
He never stays the same,
and scares the oncoming mouse.

In the darkness,
you feel all alone.
Even when,
you are in your own home.

The taste of bitterness,
fills the air.
Because you are in,
his awful lair.

You cannot see him,
but he makes his presence clear.
Even when,
you begin to fear.

In the dreary darkness,
everything is soundless.
And the smell shows,
that he is boundless.

The darkness reminds me of space,
the space outside of space,
the space where mists are drowned,
the space which is far from me.

**Rowan Cole  (10)**
**Brambletye Junior School**

# Wind

Now the wind is a
wild, angry bull,
a dangerous bull.
Clumsily tossing and
turning and trying to
break free.

Now the wind is
growing too strong,
it cannot control its rage.
The bull's ropes hold him tight.
But still he's swiftly tossing
and turning and trying to
break free.

Soon the ropes fray - *snap!*
The bull is free.
Tearing through houses
and uprooting trees in his frenzy.

But slowly he stops.
He's worn out.
So he reluctantly moves
back to his emerald-green
pastures.
The wind is calm.

**Helena Ritter  (10)**
**Brambletye Junior School**

# Winter

Winter has come.
Trees are transforming into sparkling silver statues.
Lakes changing into playgrounds of ice.
Then after a few chilly, winter days,
Fog starts to creep towards the village.
It's getting closer . . . closer . . . closer,
Wait!
It's struck, so thick, we're all blinded.
After a few hours it starts to drift away, like a lost tissue.
But the next morning flowers appear.
Trees have blossomed.
Winter is no more.

**Grace Mitchell  (11)**
**Brambletye Junior School**

# Monday

Monday again,
It's raining on Monday again,
The postman comes in the pouring rain again,
School starts on Monday, again,
It's Monday.

I walk drearily down the stairs, barely standing.
The rain still pouring like a burst pipe.
Things like this only happen on Monday.

Monday again,
It's raining on Monday again,
The postman comes in the pouring rain again,
School starts on Monday, again,
It's Monday.

I walk outside into the slashing rain, still half asleep,
The side of the street's flooding like a fast moving snake,
Things like that only happen on Monday.

Monday again,
It's raining on Monday again,
The postman comes in the pouring rain again,
School starts on Monday, again,
It's Monday.

I look outside, it's still raining,
I wonder if the rain will stop,
After a while, a shaft of light like a ray from Heaven,
Breaks into the world,
It's not Monday any more.

**Tom Wainwright  (10)**
**Brambletye Junior School**

# A Wonderful White Winter

It's a wonderful white winter.
The white carpet has been laid
On the cold, icy grass.

Wild woodland animals
Scurry along gathering food
For their forest feast.

A smell of smoke rises from the
Cottage chimney
As a fire burns bright.

It's a wonderful white winter.

**Charlotte Curran  (10)**
**Brambletye Junior School**

# The Wind

Today the wind is like a drifting ghost,
Whooshing past your face.
And the child playing on a swing,
Whooshing with enthusiasm back and forth.

Tomorrow the wind will blow searching for attention,
And shall blow and shall get depressed,
Whilst destroying all things that block its way.
Then is like a child having a tantrum.

Next week the wind shall calm, nothing to blow anymore.
The wind is like a bird now, all calm and peaceful.
Whilst the land is like a pancake, all flat and lumpy.

A shiver sweeps across the dirty, abandoned land,
Salty sand blown by the sorry wind,
Then all is still and quiet,
The wind dies down, it's gone.

**Bethany Field  (11)**
**Brambletye Junior School**

# The Man Walking Down The Street

A man was walking down the street
Like he was a drunken man
With a beer in his hand and a bag full of beer
Walking down the deserted street
No one there
Rubbish everywhere
No one to care!

The man walking down the street
Going nowhere
Walking for miles and miles
Down the isolated street
All you can hear is birds screeching
Walls crackling, just about to fall
And that's the man
Who walked down the street.

**Elis Tyre  (11)**
**Brambletye Junior School**

# The Wind's Song

The wind's song is like a smooth flow,
A smooth flow, down low.
Down low, where I am kneeling,
And out to sea, as far as I know.

The wind glides along,
Along the sea, singing a song.
The song of the blue, glittery sea,
The song of the cliffs, next to me.

The seagulls flying in the wind,
The seagulls with fluffy grey feathers.
Singing their song,
As they glide along.

The old brown leaves flying around,
Making an old rustling song.
The wind picks up over the sea,
Over the sea as far as I can see.

**Emma Sheppard (10)**
**Brambletye Junior School**

# The Seaside At Summer

The sea is a trampoline,
Bouncing up and down,
Seagulls like fish to eat,
And the smell of chips is in the air.

The salty taste is like a sour sweet,
That children like to eat,
Everyone is having fun playing around,
Eating ice cream and running round.

The slippery, slimy seaweed,
Sits there getting people's feet tangled,
Lots of children complaining,
That sand is in-between their toes.

Golden sand gets washed away,
And the beautiful sun goes down,
The beach is dark and empty now,
Everyone's gone home.

**Emma Wade  (11)**
**Brambletye Junior School**

# Dessert

Chocolate feels smooth but bumpy, it looks brown but black,
Chocolate is very tasty or very sickly, it's round or rectangular,
Chocolate is soft or hard, it's lovely melted,
Chocolate is solid or a liquid, it's lovely in a fondue.

Ice cream is white or pink, it feels smooth or fluffy,
Ice cream is cream or milk, it tastes hot or cold,
Ice cream in a tub or in a cone, it smells of strawberry or chocolate.

**Darryl Couzens (10)**
**Brambletye Junior School**

# Golf

It is only sometimes
that golf
is calm, peaceful,
but not all of the time!

Golf is a wonderful sport,
a calm sport,
a quiet sport,
the sport of golf is lovely!

The golf club is a hunter,
swinging for his dinner,
the golf ball is the prey,
being hunted for no reason at all!

The birds hear the hit,
other birds fly away,
from the trees where they sit,
they fly away.

The bird flies down the field,
escaping from him,
the hunter chases him,
with anxiety swirling inside him!

The hunter corners him on the green,
the anxiety blasts out,
and the bird is shot,
and the ball is in the hole!

**Liam Cooke (11)**
**Brambletye Junior School**

# My Grandad

We called my grandad Superman.
He once pulled a tree right out of the ground!

He knocked a wall down with his head!
He was tired afterwards; he had to go to bed.

People don't believe me, and I don't need them to.
I was there, I saw it, and I know it's true.

My grandad just adored chess.
He was much better than I have to confess.

One day he got ill and we stayed at our friends.
Mum and Dad came through the door with tears that will never end.

They sat me on the sofa with tears in each eye.
And they both let out a big, sad sigh.

Mum said Grandad wasn't with us anymore.
I knew what she meant, I felt like crying and stamping out of the door!

But Dad said something that made us all feel much better.
My grandad, my Superman, would be watching over us forever!

**Lily Jones  (9)**
**Bramley School**

# My Cat Oliver

My cat is as black at the night's sky,
His fur shimmers in the light,
His fur is as soft as cotton wool,
When you touch him he feels so silky and sleek.
My cat has glowing olive-green eyes,
He looks so cute and adorable with them,
His eyes make you want to stroke him,
But they can look scary when it's pitch-black at night.

My cat is very old but active,
He loves to chase string and other toys,
But sometimes he lies down and he purrs,
I love my cat like this.

My cat can get annoyed sometimes,
But I love my cat to bits,
I have the best cat in the world.

**Chloe Ivens  (10)**
**Cheam Common Junior School**

# First Day

Science, maths and literacy,
French, RE and ICT,
Top tucked in and never out,
Inside out and the teacher will shout.
Italy and Germany, also learning about galaxy,
Always listen when Teacher is talking,
Running down the corridor? You should be walking!
Children playing happily,
Yelling yippee and shouting with glee,
This is the playground,
The teacher wants to see.

Feeling blue, weak and poor,
Don't worry get a teacher or peer mediator
Ain't got your homework?
You're in at lunch,
And you said you'd been playing with that naughty bunch,
Well for that you can wear the old dunce.
History and geography,
This is the work we do you see.

So . . .
Got your top tucked in and not out?
Walking down the corridor?
Got your homework ready for tomorrow?
Welcome to our school ya old fellow.

**Rachel Smith  (10)**
**Cheam Common Junior School**

# Everyone

Everyone says I'm cool and funny
They like me, they love me, I can't help it
Everyone thinks I'm helpful and cute
They say I'm popular and smart too
That's what they think from their point of view
But I'm only a person!

**Milana Svaldenyte (10)**
**Cheam Common Junior School**

# Ode To My Father

Hail! to the mighty king of my heart!
You're just like a hero that is so strong,
I see you so wise and tall like King Kong.
In my soul you're very precious,
The food you make is so delicious!

You're the king of the world!
And I will always share my love and care.
The things we do, we will always be fair.

Now hear me! Now hear me!
He's my love, my care,
I dedicate this ode
To my father,
Whom I love.

**Dinah Mehnaz Ali  (11)**
**Cheam Common Junior School**

# Top Tips To Annoy Your Mum And Dad

You want to annoy your mum or dad,
Want to make them boiling mad?
Well . . .
You could use a fart machine when there's no smell,
Or you could put salt in the pepper pot,
And what about pepper in the salt pot?

You want to annoy your mum or dad,
Want to make them boiling mad?
Let's get going,
You could put make-up on Dad when he's snoring,
What about ghastly whistling
And saying there's a draught in your home
Or putting mud on Mum's best comb?

You want to annoy your mum and dad,
Want to make them boiling mad?
What about this . . .
When they ask you to do something awful, give it a miss!
Even better, squirt gooey tomato sauce in Mum's face,
Find some squirming maggots and put them in Dad's briefcase!

Want to annoy you mum or dad,
Want to make them boiling mad?
With this next one you cannot even find a tiny fault . . .
Shoot your brother from a catapult!
Or you could be a sweet kid, not their worst foe,
You could never do that could you?
No I didn't think so!

**Chloe Wall  (11)**
**Cheam Common Junior School**

# Kittens

My kittens are soft and cuddly and also very snuggly.
One is white, the other is brown,
Which gives me a happy frown.

When they snuggle down in bed,
They close their eyes and rest their heads.

When my kittens are in their big dreamworld,
They dream of stories I have told.

When the sun rises the kittens wake up,
And have a drink from their little milk cup.

One day, when my kittens are grown,
They will find a safe spot to die in peace,
Whilst we are having a midnight feast!

**Heather Phillpot (9)**
**Cheam Common Junior School**

# I'm Suffering

I'm scared every day to go to school!
Because of bullies who think they're cool,
But they're not, they're just fools,
To think it's fun to bully at school.

*I'm suffering . . . I'm suffering*

They picked on me all day,
In the end you have to pay,
That's all I've got to say.

*I'm suffering . . . I'm suffering*

I'm too scared to tell,
As they start to yell,
I can't take it anymore,
You laughed at what I wore.

*I'm suffering . . . I'm suffering*

I want to die,
I sigh and sigh,
There I just lie,
Wanting to die.

*I'm suffering . . . I'm suffering.*

**Elle Gentle  (11)**
**Cheam Common Junior School**

# Frostie The Snowman

S miling in front of me was a snowman.
N othing, nothing at all could make me forget that day.
O n that special day I made a snowman, so big,
   like a giant outside my door.
W hat did I call him? I called him Frostie, Frostie the snowman.
M aking him was fun but it was time for him to go.
A t that time when he was gone, I got unbearably sad,
   tears came down my cheeks.
N ow I have met my friends again, I am happy once more.

**Joony Han  (10)**
**Cheam Common Junior School**

# My Poor Old Gran With Only One Eye

My poor old gran with only one eye,
She looked at the ground and then looked at the sky,
She could not tell the difference! Oh my! Oh my!
My poor old gran with only one eye.

My poor old gran with only one eye.
If I wasn't around she'd have eaten a fly!
She can't tell the difference from pudding and pie,
My poor old gran with only one eye.

My poor old gran with only one eye.
She waved at a postbox and then shouted, 'Hi!'
Although I got worried, I never asked why.
My poor old gran with only one eye!

**Laura El-Bahrawy  (10)**
**Cheam Common Junior School**

# Puppies

Puppies are wonderful, puppies are great,
They put a smile on my face.
They are so cuddly and soft,
I love cuddling them to bits.

Puppies are wonderful, puppies are great,
They put a smile on my face.
They are so cute and playful.
Oh I wish I had a puppy so cuddly and cute.
Of any type, I don't really mind,
Though a Dalmatian would be nice for me.

I love puppies and I hope they love me.

**Amba Storm Corsini  (10)**
**Cheam Common Junior Sc hool**

# Anger

Anger is like a devil in blazing hot fire
Anger is a bloodthirsty, spiritual sun
Anger is the colour of my blood, the colour everyone hates.
Anger looks like an old granny's lumpy wrinkles.

Anger is like a devil's in control
Anger is like you're in a deadly coffin
Anger is bad and is like red, evil eyes gazing right at you
Anger is spicy and hot like red-hot chilli peppers.

Anger is like a devil in Hell
Anger rampages inside your body
Anger tries to escape from your soul
Anger is like a tornado taking down houses.

**Zibran Ahmed  (9)**
**Cheam Common Junior School**

# Embarrassed

E verybody is staring at me, I look down in shame
M ortified, because they are all laughing and pointing in my face
B ashful and nervous, my face has gone red
A nnoyed with myself for being a fool
R aging inside but trying to stay calm
R ude people making fun of the way I walk and talk
A wkwardly shifting in my seat, trying not to cry
S crunching up my face in disgrace, I am
S o worried about playtime, will they still be jeering?
E ating my lunch was a nightmare, people pointing and giggling
D id I actually do something wrong? Life can be so confusing.

**Emily Roach (10)**
**Cheam Common Junior School**

# Autumn

As the autumn wind whispers and blows,
Taking green leaves as he goes,
Replacing the green with the brown,
Without even turning around.

Farmers busy harvesting crops,
Before the winter curtain drops,
Animals busy gathering too,
It's the time of year with lots to do.

Baby birds have left the nest,
There is no time to rest,
Soon they'll fly far away,
For a winter holiday.

Days grow shorter every week,
Even darker as we speak,
When I get up out of bed,
The sun hasn't raised his weary head.

Autumn is a colourful time of year,
Come on now, let's all cheer,
Christmas is really, really near,
That's what we look forward to every year.

**Leah Dennis  (11)**
**Cheam Common Junior School**

# Dancing

Dancing is lots of fun
You can do tap, ballet and disco
So come and join
Be part of this brilliant fun

You can do lots
Shows and even be on stage
Everyone enjoys it
So why can't you?

**Georgia Flint  (10)**
**Cheam Common Junior School**

# December

D ecorations on the Christmas Tree
E scorting Santa to his sleigh
C hristmas carols, singing at your door
E njoying the last month of the year
M ilk and cookies on the table
B linking at the sight of Santa
E ating turkey and Christmas dinner
R eindeer on the roof of your house.

**Jamie Scarborough  (9)**
**Cheam Common Junior School**

# Homework, Homework, Homework

Homework, homework, homework,
It is so boring,
And we all hate it,
Even the teacher can admit it.
'Oh, when I was a young boy . . .'
Here comes the life story again!
'Oh yes, the dreaded homework,
That's what we used to call it,
Dreaded and evil.'

When you get home,
All you want to do is sit down and watch TV,
But what do you get . . . ?
'Oh lovely, go and do your homework,
Then you can help with the dishes.'

Homework is so time wasting,
That's what they used to say,
What's the point of it?
The dreaded
Homework,
Homework,
Homework!

**Suzy Astwood  (10)**
**Cheam Common Junior School**

# Every Time

Every time I say something another person hates me,
Every time I try to hide they always come and find me,
Every time I tell the teacher he doesn't believe me,
Every time I go to sleep I wish the night would never end!

**Elle Sinclair  (11)**
**Cheam Common Junior School**

# Fairies

Oh what beautiful fairies,
So colourful and bright,
Pink, blue, red, whatever you like,
How I like fairies glittering in the night,
Fairies so magical you'll get what you want.

**Rachel Turner  (10)**
**Cheam Common Junior School**

# Daffodils

D uring the day
A fter the sunset
F lowing side to side
F alling backwards and forwards
O ver the bushy bush as green as a grasshopper
D eadly beautiful
I n its own way
L ater and later
S uddenly they grow back again.

**Priya Patel (9)**
**Cheam Common Junior School**

# My Pet

I asked my mum:
'Can I have a pet?'
'A pet?' Mum said,
'You need to ask your dad.'

Then I asked my dad:
'Dad, can I have a pet?'
'A pet?' Dad said,
'I'm allergic to a cat.'

'Mum, Dad, I don't want a cat,
I want a dog who'll play with a ball.'

'Fine,' Mum said,
'We'll see,' said Dad,
'But I'll tell you something,
His name is Ronny and that's that.'

**Ana Popovic  (7)**
**Cheam Common Junior School**

# Nature

I wonder why the sea is blue.
I wonder why the land is green.
I wonder why the Earth is round.
I wonder why the clouds are white.

I wonder why the Earth is big.
I wonder why the Earth is turning.
I wonder why we have day and night.
I wonder why the sky is blue.

I wonder where the countries come from.
I wonder where the animals come from.
I wonder where the people come from.
I wonder where the food comes from.

I wonder why the weather changes.
I wonder why we have seasons.
I wonder why the grass is green.
I wonder why the rose has thorns.

I wonder why the trees are tall.
I wonder why the flowers are short.
I wonder why the elephants are big.
I wonder why the ants are small.

I wonder why we have sunset.
I wonder why we have midnight.
I wonder why we have midday.
I wonder why we have sunrise.

**Ryan Lee Shankar  (8)**
**Cheam Common Junior School**

# On The Turn Of A Page

Books, books, amazing books,
Can visit places where you can't look.
Have pixies, goblins and pretty fairies,
Naughty boys with elegant canaries.
Teddy bears come alive,
Belong to kids only 5.
Monsters and dragons breathing fire,
Flying carpets here to hire.
Huge genies from a lamp,
Blue-faced people going to camp.
A talking dog going on a walk,
A red goblin munching on chalk.
Wizards and witches flying on brooms,
Weird people in square-shaped rooms.
Fungus the bogeyman picking his nose,
While turning on the garden hose.
Clockwork clowns telling jokes,
A flying bicycle with fiery spokes.
All these things hidden away,
Ready to read and come out to play.

**Lydia Wood (9)**
**Cheam Common Junior School**

# My Fat, Furry Pussycat

I have a cat called Jasmine,
She's very cute and fluffy.
She feels like a cuddly cushion,
And she's big and puffy.

She loves to nick your chicken,
Lots and lots and lots.
When you put ice cream out,
She cleans it up like pots.

Jasmine's black and white all over,
With lovely thick fur.
When she goes to sleep at night,
She loves to loudly purr.

I love her so much,
And I say she's the best in the world.
When she's also in bed at night,
I see her snug and curled.

**Katie Knowles  (9)**
**Cheam Common Junior School**

# My Parents

My parents are like my best friend,
They will look after me till the end.
I will love them forever,
We will always have great parties together.
My parents teach me every day,
Making sure I don't run away.
They will care for me,
Taking photos with all smiles and cheers,
Putting me to bed saying, 'Goodnight, my dear.'

**Louise Man (8)**
**Cheam Common Junior School**

# Dancing Violets

I wandered through the beautiful woods
As slow as a snail,
When suddenly something caught my eye,
A crowd of purple violets,
Dancing in the gentle breeze.
Every other flower seemed to be watching,
Admiring the beautiful dance.
Continuous, like stars in the galaxy,
They seemed never to end,
Nearly a hundred I think I spotted,
Or maybe much, much, more.
Now when I pass a crowd of violets,
I bow down as if to say *hello!*

**Sophie Choi  (9)**
**Cheam Common Junior School**

# Oranges

Oranges, oranges, oranges,
Oranges look as pretty as a sweet rose in the sun.

Oranges taste so mouth-watering, I fall asleep.
Oranges feel soft like a silky baby lamb.
Oranges smell like a pretty perfume, sweet as a sunflower.

**Millie Lucy Nelson (7)**
**Cheam Common Junior School**

# My Dog Danny

My dog Danny is grey and white.
He has eyes as brown as a Malteser.
He sleeps on my bed and cuddles me tight.
He has lots of doggy friends and loves to play.
He loves to walk and I wish,
Just sometimes, that he could talk.

**Rosie Keenan  (8)**
**Cheam Common Junior School**

# Oranges And Bananas

Oranges feel as rough as a rope.
Oranges look like min footballs.
Oranges taste as juicy as a drink.
Oranges smell as healthy as water.

Bananas look like the shining moon.
Bananas taste as nice as a chocolate bar.
Bananas feel as fresh as flowers.
Bananas smell really nutritious.

**Alfie Broadbent  (8)**
**Cheam Common Junior School**

# The Beginning Of Spring - Haiku

Birds sing, flowers bloom
A carpet of crocuses
With blossom for you.

**Hannah Oxford  (10)**
**Educare Small School**

# Autumn Is Here - Haiku

Sweet, hot chocolate
The moon and stars bright, I'm cold,
For autumn is here.

**Saskia Prabhavalkar (9)**
**Educare Small School**

# Summer Fun - Haiku

Happy holidays
Lots of sun, sand and warm sea
Green leaves and tall trees.

**Arthur Vie  (9)**
**Educare Small School**

# I Like Tortoises

Its skin is wrinkly,
Its shell is hard.
It may not be furry,
It may be very old,
But I like it,
However old it is.

**Lily Vie  (8)**
**Educare Small School**

# Rabbits

A rabbit is a medium-sized creature.
It's a mammal.
It's very bouncy.
It's fast and
It likes carrots.

**Gabrielle Prabhavalkar  (7)**
Educare Small School

# Rabbits

Rabbits are . . .
Fast, quick, speedy, bouncy.
They love eating carrots.
Rabbits come in different colours.

**Ben Westerby-Cox (8)**
Educare Small School

# Tortoises Are Nice

Tortoises are not fast,
But even so they are nice.
They don't bite,
But they are old,
Like they have come out of a mould,
But don't be fooled,
Tortoises are nice.

**Billy Smith  (8)**
**Educare Small School**

## ...asons

Spring is a clean start
Flowers starting to grow
The beginning of the year
Beauty starting to show

Summer so, so heavenly
Clear sky, crystal-blue
Seaside sand, warm nights
Everything you want to do

Autumn with a weather change
The auburn gold leaves
Swaying through the wind
Falling off the trees

Winter weather, freezing cold
But excitement high not low
Because what arrives with winter
Is the fluffy *snow!*

**Ellie Payton  (9)**
**Esher Church School**

# The Mermaid

The mermaid swam across the pool,
Water drifted through her hair,
Banged her head upon a wall,
This gave her quite a shocking scare.

She's not used to enclosed water,
She prefers it running free,
She's used to the gift life brought her,
Not like the gift life brought to you and me.

Her gift was a shining, scaly tail,
Used to swim around the world,
Her head hurt so she gave a wail,
And out of our school pool she hurled.

She sat upon the slippy tiles,
She wished that she was back home,
But she'd have to travel miles,
And how she longed for the frothy foam.

She heard her home calling her,
But alas, she had a broken bone,
She said goodbye to the land of the mer,
Poor, poor mermaid, afraid and alone.

**Georgina Morris  (9)**
**Esher Church School**

# My Senses

I like to look at . . .
The playground with lots of children chilling out,
The vegetable vines zooming up to the sky,
The sparkling sky that shines so bright.

I like to listen to . . .
The paint splatting on the gloriously clean paper,
The children eating a lot of crunchy food like crisps,
The children laughing so hard they cough.

I like the smell of . . .
The sweet, fresh air in the playground,
The dinner food wafting through the air,
The fresh flowers growing up to the sky.

I like to feel . . .
The rough playground when you run over it,
The soft books when they have been open for a long time,
The smooth surface of the whiteboard.

I like to taste . . .
The lovely sandwiches, sweet tasting with cheese, pickle and onions,
The French fries and plums for my lunch.

**Cameron Bullen  (7)**
**Gilbert Scott Junior School**

# My Senses

I like to look at . . .
The glamorous teachers in the classroom.
The whiteboard shining in the classroom.
The pictures in the beautiful staffroom.

I like to listen to . . .
The beautiful loud birds.
The teachers talking quietly in the dinner hall.
The children talking in class.

I like the smell of . . .
Fresh fruit in the dinner hall.
Lovely custard spattering in the pot.
Pizza on people's plates in the dinner hall.

I like to feel . . .
My friend's hands when in the playground.
The lovely trees covering the field.
Cakes at home.

I like to taste . . .
Lovely chocolate sparkling in my mouth.
The lovely grass growing on the field.
School dinners from the dinner hall.

**Richard Pingling  (8)**
**Gilbert Scott Junior School**

# My Senses

I like to look at . . .
The vegetables that grow smoothly.
The books in the library with lots of information.
The fish tank in the classroom.

I like to listen to . . .
The wind zipping through the playground.
The children talking when they're working in pairs.
The teachers talking in the playground.

I like the smell of . . .
Mrs Daw's perfume when I am hugging her.
The lovely flowers out of the classroom window.
The pizza cooking in the dinner hall.

I like to feel . . .
The smooth tables in the classroom.
The rough paper when I am writing.
The smooth books when I am choosing a book.

I like to taste . . .
The sweet custard in the dinner hall,
The sweet juice when I have a special lunch.
The fresh fruits in the dinner hall.

**Kamilla Yarmolenko (7)**
**Gilbert Scott Junior School**

# Weather

Suddenly,
The rain fell down
And made the ground wet.

Noisily,
The wind blew around the school
While the children stayed inside.

Silently,
The clouds flew by
And birds flew past me.

Quickly,
The leaves floated to earth
And landed softly
Without making a sound.

Gently,
The grass moved
In the wind.

Luckily,
The sun shone brightly
And made everything look cheerful.

**Emily Raeburn  (9)**
**Gilbert Scott Junior School**

# My Picnic

We've . . .
Banana cake, apple cake,
Cheesecake,
Choose now quickly!

I want jelly!

There's . . .
Apple juice, orange juice,
Berry juice, peach juice,
Hurry up, take one,
Please.

I want jelly!

There's . . .
Banana, apple,
Orange, berries,
Just take one!
Come on now.

I . . . want . . . jelly!

**Alfie Smidt (8)**
**Gilbert Scott Junior School**

# Racing Cars

Quickly,
The racing car started the race.

Speedily,
They sped round the corner.

Dangerously,
The car hit the curb.

Suddenly,
All the cars crashed together.

Unbelievably,
A car tipped over and burst into flames.

Madly,
The driver flew out the window.

Fortunately,
The driver had his headgear on.

Luckily,
He survived the dangerous car crash.

**Travis Mendoza  (8)**
**Gilbert Scott Junior School**

# In The Sky

Slowly,
The clouds moved high above the Earth.

Quickly,
The plane flew higher in the sky.

Speedily,
The rocket took the children into space.

Swiftly,
The kite flew into the air.

Noisily,
The helicopter hovered in the sky.

Delicately,
The bird landed on the tree branch.

Brightly,
The moon gave light to the people below.

Brilliantly,
The stars shone in the dark sky.

**Aylin Yilmaz  (8)**
**Gilbert Scott Junior School**

# Animals

Slowly,
The tortoise won the race.
He was very pleased.

Luckily,
The rabbit found a carrot.
He wasn't hungry anymore.

Quietly,
The hedgehog slowly went to sleep.

Quickly,
The bird flew into her nest,
Hiding from the cat.

Loudly,
The naughty dog barked,
And her owner told her off.

Suddenly,
The cat jumped onto my mum's lap.
She got a fright.

Proudly,
The fox ran across my garden
And into my neighbour's garden.

**Ria Willis  (9)**
**Gilbert Scott Junior School**

# Animals

Quickly,
The squirrel grabbed the acorns I gave him.

Luckily,
The mole found a place to dig a hole.

Proudly,
The rabbit sat next to the pile of carrots he had found.

Silently,
The mouse sneaked up to the cheese.

Busily,
The dog chewed on his bone that he saved for emergencies.

Sadly,
The hare lost the race to a tortoise.

**Kwame Obiri-Addai (8)**
**Gilbert Scott Junior School**

# The Boy

Quickly,
The boy rushed into class.

Slowly,
The boy walked down the corridor.

Angrily,
The teacher told off the boy.

Proudly,
The boy sang a Christmas carol.

Carelessly,
The boy tore his work.
Luckily,
The boy won the school raffle.

Suddenly,
The boy tripped as he jumped over the wall.

Noisily,
The boy played in the playground with his friends.

Sadly,
The boy swept the floor.

Carefully,
The boy ran out into the playground.

Joyfully,
The boy skipped out of school,
He was going home at last.

**Levi Campbell (8)**
**Gilbert Scott Junior School**

# The Crime Fighters

Swiftly,
Batman soared across the sky to his Batlab.

Stealthily,
Violet crept down the road to school.

Aggressively,
The Crimson Chin fought the Bronze Kneecap in the bank.

Silently,
Spider-Man climbed up the wall to Mary-Jane's house.

Madly,
The Hulk turned green in the yard.

Luckily,
Superman destroyed the meteor falling from the sky.

Smartly,
The Avatar outwitted the Spirit Monster.

**Nathan Dunford  (9)**
**Gilbert Scott Junior School**

# Dinner

We've got . . .
Beans, bacon, chicken rolls,
Jacket potatoes too,
Hurry up and choose now,
These are just for you.

I want a Galaxy.

We've got . . .
Sandwiches, crisps, chicken rolls,
Cheese rolls . . .
Come on now,
Hurry up and take one, please.

I want a Galaxy.

We've got . . .
Pizza, sausages,
Chips, chicken . . .
Hurry up please,
Take one now.

I want a Galaxy.

We've got . . .
Jam doughnuts, bread and jam,
Chocolate spread, as well,
Hurry up please
And choose the one you want!

I want a Galaxy!

**Kyle Williams  (9)**
**Gilbert Scott Junior School**

# I Wish . . .

I wish I could be small enough
To be able to climb up trees.

I wish I could sleep all night
Under a roof on top of a birds' nest.

I wish I could be a dragonfly
And be a great flyer and be colourful.

I wish I could hide inside a bluebell's stem
To stay away from madness.

I wish I could wear a snail's shell
To keep me cosy.

I wish I could be a diary
To keep secrets from others.

I wish I could be a panda
To have a thick coat.

I wish I could be a professional player
To score volleys over the keeper's head.

I wish I could have donkey teeth
So they do not fall out.

I wish I could be money
For people to spend.

**Clayton Ryan  (8)**
**Gilbert Scott Junior School**

# I Wish

I wish I could be a millionaire
So I could buy a big house.

I wish I had a Bugatti Veiron
To drive very fast.

I wish I could travel in time
To go back to 1942.

I wish I could live forever
To see what happens in the future.

I wish I could have a motorbike
To go through small gaps.

I wish I had a horse
To gallop round a field.

I wish I could control the world
So everyone had to do what I say.

I wish I had all the James Bond cars
To play with.

I wish I could cuddle my hamster all day
Because he is so sweet.

I wish I could travel the world
And be very clever.

**Jake King  (8)**
**Gilbert Scott Junior School**

# I Wish . . .

I wish I could be small enough
To drive a toy car as a normal car.

I wish I could stay awake all the time
And play football with a marble all day.
And play the miniature PS2 all night.

I wish I could be a small toy
And not even get hurt by bigger people.

I wish I could be Cristiano Ronaldo
To score a hat-trick every match.

I wish I could make a dream team
To have all the best footballers.
I wish I could be the best footballer
To win loads of matches.

I wish I could be a boy
Who always keeps the best Top Trumps, never, ever loses them.

I wish I could be a footballer
To score goals non-stop.

I wish I could be a boy who always gets his own way
To do everything I want.

I wish I could be a boy who always stays
To never, ever die and waste time with funerals.

**Jacob Moody  (8)**
**Gilbert Scott Junior School**

# I Wish . . .

I wish I could run quickly
Like a calm cheetah.

I wish I could fly
With fragile, fluttering fairy wings
To see the world from a bird's-eye view.

I wish I could bounce like a ball
And see the smiles of the children
That would play with me.

I wish I could fit
Into the nooks and crannies of an attic.

I wish I could be a wise owl
With wide wings to soar.

I wish I could be a tulip
Like a colourful cup
And bloom in the spring.

I wish I could be a trumpet
And play in a jazz band.

I wish I could be a grasshopper
And hop through the lush, green grass.

I wish I could be a lantern
And shine brightly to give light.

I wish I could be a sweet smile
Like a flower blooming for the world to see.

**Elysia Beaumont (8)**
Gilbert Scott Junior School

# I Wish

I wish I could be fast enough
To run the Croydon marathon.

I wish I could fly all night
And around the world in 80 seconds non-stop whatsoever.

I wish I could be  a president
To give for sale houses to the homeless people.

I wish I could be brave enough
To run through a fire and save people
Then run back out again.

I wish I could be a miniature ant
To warn ants of danger.

I wish I could be a slithery snake
To move around and do nothing all day.

I wish I could wear a snail's shell
To hide from big dogs.

I wish I could be blossom on a tree
So I could be fresh and happy.

I wish I could sleep all night
In a cosy, warm bed.

I wish I could be a dragonfly
And see the world from up high.

**Fabian Thomas  (8)**
**Gilbert Scott Junior School**

# Dreams

A dog dreams
Of a juicy bone and a cosy basket.
A sky dreams
Of a warm sun with white clouds.
A skateboard dreams
Of an opportunity to go to a skate park.
A house dreams
Of having visitors to decorate it.
A waterfall dreams
Of a brave swordfish to scratch his back.
A computer dreams
Of sending emails to friends.
A mouse dreams
Of a house full of cheese.
A child dreams
Of a visit to the park to have fun.
A poem dreams
Of a happy ending
To make everyone happy.

**Kofi Achina  (9)**
**Gilbert Scott Junior School**

# Mysteries

Why are teachers sometimes moany?
Why are tramps always lonely?
Why do fast cars cause a crash?
Why does chickenpox cause a rash?

Why do weddings have a song?
Why are snakes always long?
Why do some men go to jail?
Why do postmen send our mail?

Why does chocolate taste so nice?
Why are some people scared of mice?
Why do matches have to end?
Why do shoes need a mend?

Why are most pigs always pink?
Why do people have to think?
Why do people eat chicken?
Why are dogs always licking?

**Eniz Ibrahim  (10)**
**Gilbert Scott Junior School**

# Mysteries

Why do mums always moan?
Why do dogs chew on bones?
Why do thieves like to steal phones?
Why do zombies always groan?

Why do people like chocolate dips?
Why do snakes not have lips?
Why do puddles make you slip?
Why do fat people have lots of chips?

Why are people sometimes shy?
Why do people like a lot of pie?
Why do birds fly so high?
Why do kids always lie?

Why do people play football?
Why do girls like the mall?
Why do people hate to fall?
Why do babies always drool?

**Alexander Sattar  (10)**
**Gilbert Scott Junior School**

# Mysteries

Why do teachers always groan?
Why do children always moan?
Why do scientists make inventions?
Why don't children pay attention?

Why are lights on at night?
Why do kids play with kites?
Why is space always black
Why do dogs chase cats?

Why are houses always nice?
Why is Antarctica full of ice?
Why are actors full of fame?
Why are tramps always lame?

Why are banks full of cash?
Why do cars sometimes crash?
Why is grass always green?
Why are head teachers always mean?

**Antonio Lising  (10)**
**Gilbert Scott Junior School**

# Mysteries

Why do children always moan?
Why do teachers always groan?
Why do dogs need their paws?
Why do we need any laws?

Why do flowers grow so slow?
Why do nans always sew?
Why do parents always talk?
Why do dogs like to go for a walk?

Why do children need to sleep?
Why do sirens go *beep, beep, beep?*
Why does water have no taste?
Why do we brush our teeth with toothpaste?

Why do birds always sing?
Why do phones have to ring?
Why do babies always cry?
Why are people sometimes shy?

**Jasmin Hayward (10)**
**Gilbert Scott Junior School**

# Mysteries

Why does water look blue?
Why do dogs do a poo?
Why do people use glue?
Why do socks come in twos?

Why do girls have long hair?
Why do people eat pears?
Why are children told what to wear?
Why do shoes come in pairs?

Why do people live in a house?
Why are people scared of a mouse?
Why does water make you wet?
Why do men like to bet?

Why do tramps smell so bad?
Why are some people so sad?
Why do people grow flowers?
Why do we have so many towers?

**Shannon White  (10)**
**Gilbert Scott Junior School**

# Mysteries

Why are cars so fast?
Why is the sky so vast?
Why do fishes have scales?
Why are females weaker than males?
Why are babies so small?
Why do people play football?
Why do people play in snow?
Why do people have a big toe?

**Bobby Hall (9)**
**Gilbert Scott Junior School**

# Mysteries

Why do dogs bark so much?
Why does snow feel cold to touch?

Why does fire feel so hot?
Why do people talk a lot?

Why do children have to learn?
Why do people have to earn?

Why is there always traffic?
Why do people like a graphic?

Why do people have a head?
Why do we go to bed?

Why do people make tea?
Why do people have to see?

**Tiffany Morant  (10)**
**Gilbert Scott Junior School**

# Outside My Window

Outside my window
A willow tree stands all alone
In the twinkling snow.
Suddenly children's footprints become
Words on the white sheet of paper,
A snowball comes flying across the sky,
Hits the trunk of the willow tree.
The crystal snowflakes stop falling,
The snow starts to melt into cold water,
Children standing wet,
They run inside.

**Hollie Nixon (10)**
**Gilbert Scott Junior School**

# Boxing

Love of boxing was Rocky's life,
It meant as much as his dear wife.
His son did train but didn't work hard,
He gave it up and threw in the card.

Rocky kept strong and visited his wife,
Though sadly only in spirit
As she had lost her life.
He struggles at times to focus on his goal,
But belief and hard work
Were his best friends and soul.

He fought well
But sadly lost,
Rocky now knew
That fighting had a cost.

**Tyler Pepperell (10)**
**Gilbert Scott Junior School**

# Mysteries

Why do people look?
Why do we read a book?
Why do we have to learn?
Why do fires burn?

Why do birds have feet?
Why do we eat meat?
Why do we cry?
Why do we have to die?

**Glen Wright (10)**
**Gilbert Scott Junior School**

# If

*(Inspired by 'If' by Rudyard Kipling)*

If the teacher is always shouting at you,
Try to be good for the day.
If you don't bring toys in; they won't be lost.
If you don't get out of your seat,
Or sharpen your pencil,
You will get more work done.

If you bring the right PE kit in
You will enjoy it more.
If you forget to do corridor duty
More children will get in.
If you practise your spellings
Or your time tables
You will get them all right.

You will always achieve in school
And what's more
You will become a man.

**Ashley Allen  (10)**
**Gilbert Scott Junior School**

# Teacher, Teacher

Teacher, teacher,
come here fast
I've won a medal
at last.

Teacher, teacher
I can't hear
I've got a problem
with my ear.

Teacher, teacher
come here quick
I have been
terribly sick.

Teacher, teacher
I'm going to faint
because I'm allergic
to the red paint.

**Maisie Billingham (10)**
**Gilbert Scott Junior School**

# If

*(Inspired by 'If' by Rudyard Kipling)*

If you can read a book,
Without asking for a meaning.
Or you can complete a sum,
Without looking at someone else's answer.
If you can walk down the corridor,
Without tripping someone up.
Or you can write a story,
Without making a mistake.

If you can play in the sand,
Without chucking it at your friend.
Or you can eat your lunch
Without starting a food fight.
If you can log onto the computer
Without it crashing.
Or you can change into your PE kit
Without missing half the lesson.

Yours is the school and the pupils in it,
And what is more, you'll achieve, my child.

**Bethany Dunn (10)**
**Gilbert Scott Junior School**

# The Day That The CD Player Broke Down

It was worse than being cold,
It was worse than growing old,
It was worse than being told.

*The day that the CD player broke down!*

My mum attempted to repair it,
But it wasn't worth it,
We tried and tried to fix it.

*The day that the CD player broke down!*

My mum said, 'Make me a cup of coffee,'
But I was eating my toffee,
And drinking my banoffee.

*I'm afraid the coffee got spilt over the CD player!*

**Brandon Johnson  (10)**
**Gilbert Scott Junior School**

# The Day My Computer Broke Down

It was worse than an earthquake, worse than war,
Worse than a little finger stuck in a door,
Worse than the worst ever worst thing before.

*The day my computer broke down!*

My brother attempted to give it first aid,
We told it we loved it, its licence was paid,
We cried and we whimpered, we knelt down and prayed.

*The day my computer broke down!*

Instead we decided to visit our aunt,
'Lend us your computer,' we said. ''Fraid I can't,
This morning your uncle thought it was a plant
And watered it, so . . .'

*I'm afraid the computer drowned!*

**Shannon Mills  (11)**
**Gilbert Scott Junior School**

# If

If you can wake up at an early rate
And go to school and not be late.

If you can pay up the money you owe
And never, ever get a letter sent home.

If you can follow an instruction given
And keep your negative feeling about it hidden.

If you can manage to eat your without going red
And eat your food at your own pace without rushing instead.

If you can avoid playing football on the playground
or being scolded with dread,
and play something else like basket ball, netball,
or cricket instead.

If you can safely and carefully walk home
Even in the dark when you are alone.

Then you have achieved the most
And in addition you are a success
My friend.

**Arjunn Senthilnathan  (11)**
**Gilbert Scott Junior School**

# The Day Arsenal Beat Chelsea

Henry shot a drill
It made Chelsea look to kill
The score was now one-nil

The day Arsenal beat Chelsea

Chelsea were on track
They scored on their attack
A nice goal by Ballack

The day Arsenal beat Chelsea

Walcott's on the run
His, it was a stun
The score was now two-one

The day Arsenal beat Chelsea

Arsenal lost their guard
Consequences were hard
A big goal for Lampard

The day Arsenal beat Chelsea

For Chelsea it was great
For Arsenal's growing fate
The score at level rate

The day Arsenal beat Chelsea

Terry tackled hard
Penalty - red card
A goal, Chelsea were scared!

The day Arsenal beat Chelsea!

**Jonathan Williamson-Taylor (10)**
**Gilbert Scott Junior School**

# Mysteries

Why do stars shine at night?
Why are calculators always right?
Why do hairs grow so slow?
Why do fans always blow?

Why do girls have long hair?
Why do shoes come in pairs?
Why do statues stand so still?
Why do people get ill?

Why do dads always drink?
Why do people always blink?
Why do dogs chew bones?
Why do people fall over stones?

Why do children eat sweets?
Why do people have smelly feet?
Why do dogs chase cats?
Why do people wear hats?

**Ellie Hale (10)**
**Gilbert Scott Junior School**

# Feelings

I'm as happy as a football player scoring a goal.
As sad as a person falling into a hole.
As upset as a very small person.

I'm as livid as a boy getting his ball nicked.
As cross as a man with people that are messing his hall up.
As terrified as a boy in the swimming pool.
As petrified as a person who fell over.

As disgusted as a teacher seeing a boy punch someone.
As happy as a boy eating his favourite lunch.
As dead as a man with no head.
As bored as a boy that got sent to his bed.

Nice feelings.

**George Kenton**
**Green Wrythe Primary School**

# As Upset As . . .

As upset as a dog with no one to stroke it.
As upset as a football match with no ball to play with.
As upset as a kid with no mum to cuddle.
As upset as a cop when he can't catch the robber.
As upset as a toilet with no one to clean it.
As upset as a man with no wife to kiss.

**Mitchell Murdoch (7)**
**Green Wrythe Primary School**

# All Sorts Of Feelings

As amazed as a little boy in the snow.
As glad as a man winning tickets to a football club.
As sad as the loser in a 15km race.
As proud as a rugby player shooting the poles.
As unhappy as if I had pinned myself twice in the leg.
As grumpy as a bear chased by a person.
As quiet as a mouse.
As cute as a kitten with nice ears.
As tired as a boy sleeping on the floor.
As miserable as a scientist destroying his own invention.
As painful as breaking your leg in a football premier final.

**Ben Honey**
**Green Wrythe Primary School**

# Feelings

As happy as a pig that's rolling in muck.
As happy as a man who is very rich.
As ill as a dog who has eaten too many treats.
As cross as a man who doesn't clean up.
As sad as a child who is poor.
As angry as a cow without any milk.
As excited as a boy who is going to Disneyland.
As upset as a cat who has no fish.
As anxious as a boy on his first day at school.

**Joshua Garrod (8)**
**Green Wrythe Primary School**

# I Feel

I am as amazed . . .
as a child when it has seen its first sunset.

As amazed . . .
as a monkey when it eats its first banana.

As amazed . . .
as the sun when it has sent its first rays to Earth.

As amazed . . .
As a book when someone has written their first word in it.

That's how amazed I am.

**Charli Barrie  (8)**
**Green Wrythe Primary School**

# I'm Feeling

I'm as sad as a pony with no one to ride it.
I'm as sad as a bug with no one to play with.

I'm as sad as a tiger with no stripes.

I'm as grumpy as a camel with the hump.
I'm as grumpy as a horse that will not jump.
I'm as grumpy as a dog that's guarding its food.

I'm as happy as a runner that's just won a race.
I'm as happy as a frog jumping up and down.
I'm as happy as a pupil that's just won a golden ticket prize.

I'm as lonely as a dragon with no one to pat it.
I'm as lonely as a dog with no one to stroke it.
I'm as lonely as a stable with no horse to live in it.

So that's how I feel!

**Florence Harris**
**Green Wrythe Primary School**

# As Excited As . . .

As excited as a tree with someone to climb it.
As excited as song with someone to mime it.

As excited as a finger with something to point at.
As excited as a spider with something to climb on.

As excited as a mint with someone to eat it.
As excited as a friend who gave me a hint.

As excited as a chair with someone to sit on it.
As excited as a boxer with something to hit.

As excited as a cupboard with something in it.
As excited as a pen with some ink in it.

As excited as some fruit with someone to eat it.
As excited as a person who eats meat.

**Amy Fountain  (7)**
**Green Wrythe Primary School**

# Feelings

As angry as a wolf.
As angry as a man who gets wound up by his child.
As petrified as the dark with owls inside.
As sick as a dog that never gets fed.
As happy as a cat who jumps around like mad.
As lonely as a bath that doesn't get run.
As sad as a dentist who lost all his teeth.
As tired as a boy who collapsed on the floor.
As angry as a crocodile who gobbles you up.
As sad as a chick with no one to care for it.

**Chelsie Gumble**
**Green Wrythe Primary School**

# Feelings

As sad as a rabbit with no hole to live in.
As upset as a phonic with no one to say it.
As lonely as a baby with no one to care for it.
As bored as a teacher with no class to teach.
As exhausted as a ghost that's just retired.
As cross as a crocodile with no water to live in.
As ecstatic as a chimpanzee with lots of trees to play and live in.

**Ellie Colvin  (9)**
**Green Wrythe Primary School**

# As Angry As . . .

As angry as an Easter bunny with no Easter eggs.
As angry as a child with no homework.
As angry as a dog with no bone.
As angry as a teacher with no work.
As angry as a rabbit with no carrot to eat.
As angry as a mum with your playroom untidy.
As angry as a customer with no food to eat.
As angry as a vampire with nobody to scare.
As angry as me when I can't get to sleep.
As angry as a dad with no money from work.
As angry as a Chelsea fan with no match today.
As angry as a horse with no sugar cubes.
As angry as a cat with no cat food.

**Laura Allen  (7)**
**Green Wrythe Primary School**

# Feelings

As exhausted as a footballer
who has just come back from a match.
As tired as a person
who has played a very long game of catch.

As angry as a cat
that can't catch a mouse.
As grumpy as a person
who has been locked up in a house.

As bored as a person
who has been in a house ill.
As furious as a rich person
that has to work in a mill.

As bored as a flower
with no bud.
As angry as a pig
with no mud.

As shy as a person
with a new guest.
As cross as a little boy
who has been tricked by a pest.

As upset as a person
with only one chick.
As wicked as a witch
flying on a broomstick.

As livid as an adult
covered in feelings.
Thank you for reading
my poem about *feelings!*

**Rhys Smith  (9)**
**Green Wrythe Primary School**

# Lonely

As lonely as an elephant with no one to play with.
As lonely as a bath with no one to run it.
As lonely as a giraffe with no scarf to wrap around his neck.
As lonely as monkey with no furry skin.
As lonely as boat with no one to row it.
As lonely as a cow with no one to milk it.
As lonely as a dog with no one to stroke it.
As lonely as a pig with no mud to roll in.
As lonely as boy with no one to play with.
As lonely as sheepdog with no sheep to round up.
As lonely as a vampire with no one to scare.
As lonely as glasses with no one to wear them.
As lonely as a tree with no leaves.
As lonely as a book with no one to write in it.
As lonely as a T-shirt with no one to wear it.

**Daisy Hunt (7)**
**Green Wrythe Primary School**

# As Lonely As . . .

As lonely as a chicken with no one to lay eggs for.
As lonely as the Easter bunny with no one to find his eggs.
As heartbroken as dog with no one to have puppies with.
As lonely as a monkey with no one to have baby monkeys with.
As lonely as a sock with no one to wear it.
As lonely as a pencil with no one to write with it.
As lonely as a potion with no one to do magic with it.

**Bradd Healy  (9)**
**Green Wrythe Primary School**

# As . . .

As clear as crystal.
As neat as a pin.
As pure as snow.
As dusty as a bin.

As dry as dust.
As high as a kite.
As clean as a whistle.
As bright as a light.

As gentle as a lamb.
As easy as A, B, C.
As hard as rock.
Just like 1, 2, 3.

As tricky as monkeys.
As wise as an owl.
As good as gold.
As soft as a towel.

As happy as a lark.
As loud as a bull.
As fat as a pig.
As easy to tell.

As smooth as silk.
As slow as a snail.
As cold as milk.
As shiny as a trail.

As soft as a pillow.
As happy as a clown.
As stiff as a board.
As gold as a crown.

**Katie Davis-Sullivan (8)**
**Green Wrythe Primary School**

# I Am . . .

As fit as a fiddle.
As mad as a goat.
As thin as a pin.
As nice as a note.

As dumb as an ox.
As fat as a boat.
As drunk as a lord.
As smart as a fox.

**Hayden Berriedale-Pocock  (9)**
**Green Wrythe Primary School**

# As . . .

As funny as hyena.
As bumpy as a tree.
As beautiful as a lady.
As fat as pastry.

As dark as mud.
As clean as snow.
As cold as ice.
As quick as my little toe.

As wet as a slug.
As smelly as a skunk.
As bright as a light.
As tidy as a bunk.

As happy as can be.
As lonely as 1, 2, 3.
As hard as A, B, C.
As slippery as the sea.

**Billie-Jo Morgan  (8)**
**Green Wrythe Primary School**

# Rachel's Simile Poem

As yummy as chocolate
when someone eats it.
As nice as a flower
when someone sniffs it.
As happy as a puppy
when someone strokes it.

As black as coal
when someone burns it.
As happy as a teddy
with someone to care for it.
As sad as a kitten
without a mother to love it.

**Rachel O'Neill (9)**
**Green Wrythe Primary School**

# My Similes

As wise as an owl.
As slow as a snail.
As white as snow.
As hard as nails.

As thin as a toothpick.
As soft as a mitten.
As pure as snow.
As weak as a kitten.

As busy as a bee.
As crazy as a loon.
As clear as crystal.
As bight as the moon.

As thick as snow.
As black as coal.
As hard as nails.
As ugly as a mole.

As soft as mittens.
As a name called Rick.
As cute as a kitten.
As thick as a brick.

**Caitlin Logue  (8)**
**Green Wrythe Primary School**

# Evan's Poem

As blind as a bat.
As strong as an ox.
As cute as a cat.
As dark as a box.

As big as an elephant.
As leggy as an octopus.
As clever as a teacher.
As weird as a platypus.

As good as gold.
As rectangular as a flag.
As clever as a pupil.
As mad as a bag.

As heavy as a stone.
As bright as a light.
As weird as a bone.
As dark as the night.

As square as a pillow.
As hard as a table.
As long as as a willow.
As messy as a stable.

As sticky as a label,
As slimy as a worm.
As annoying as a cable.
As dirty as a germ.

As soft as a ball.
As yellow as a book.
As dumb as a doorknob.
As cool as my look.

**Evan Hewes (9)**
**Green Wrythe Primary School**

# As Happy . . .

As poor as a boy.
As strong as an ox.
As cute as a puppy.
As smart as a fox.

As happy as a fish.
As square as a bat.
As silky as me.
As black as a bat.

As sad as a bag.
As cross as me.
As hot as a pan.
As bad as a flea.

As happy as a cat.
As busy as a bee.
As furry as a mat.
As lovely as me.

**Charlotte Gant (7)**
**Green Wrythe Primary School**

# My Irritated Poem

As clear as crystal.
As cold as ice.
As clean as a whistle.
As quick as mice.

As cool as a cat.
As blind as a mole.
As dirty as a mat.
As big as a hole.

As black as coal.
As white as snow.
As ugly as a mole.
As naughty as the word no.

As thick as a brick.
As noisy as a tick.
As naughty as a lick.
As a name called Mick.

As weak as a kitten.
As soft as a mitten.
As permanent as written.
As hurtful as a kitten.

**Paige Waller  (7)**
**Green Wrythe Primary School**

# As Busy . . .

As drunk as a lord,
As dry as a bone.
As right as rain.
As pointy as a comb.

As dull as dishwater.
As fit as a fiddle.
As neat as a pin.
As clean as a whistle.

As busy as mum.
As crazy as a loon.
As buzzy as a bee.
As big as the moon.

**Charlie-Jade Mills (9)**
**Green Wrythe Primary School**

# As Happy As . . .

I'm as happy as a builder making money.
I'm as happy as bird who has just given birth.
I'm as happy as a bear eating honey.
I'm as happy as the Earth.
I'm as happy as God who made me good.
I'm as happy as a hero who climbed out of a pit.
I'm as happy as a man who has good children.
I'm as happy as a chair with someone to sit on it.
I'm as happy as a man who's got a job.
I'm as happy as a woman who loves to shop.
I'm as happy as a banana with someone to eat it.
I'm as happy as a butcher with some meat to chop.

**Brandon Pembroke (9)**
**Green Wrythe Primary School**

# Simile Poem

As clean as a whistle.
As smart as a fox.
As light as a feather.
As strong as an ox.
As busy as a cat on a hot tin roof.
As cold as ice.
As smooth as silk.
As white as rice.
As cute as a cupcake.
As crazy as a loon.
As busy as a beaver.
As cool as a racoon.
As busy as a bee.
As fast as a dog.
As little as a mouse.
As still as a log.
As dry as a bone.
As small as a cat.
As fast as a cheetah.
As fine as an ice cream cone.
As tall as a tree.
As big as a land.
As cold as ice cream.
As sad as you fall.
As deep as a well.
As still as a wall.
As kind as a mother.
As fit as an ox.
As cute as a puppy.
As creepy as a fox.

**Casey Wright  (9)**
**Green Wrythe Primary School**

# As . . .

As fat as a pig.
As cute as a kitten.
As happy as a clown.
As soft as a mitten.

As old as the hills.
As easy as pie.
As white as snow.
As fat as a lie.

As poor as dirt.
As clear as mud.
As still as death.
As loud as a thud!

As round as a button.
As clear as crystal.
As bright as day.
As clean as a whistle.

As clear as a bell.
As plain as day.
As flat as a pancake.
And my birthday is in May.

**Shannon Holmes  (8)**
**Green Wrythe Primary School**

# Similes

As poor as a church mouse.
As strong as an ox.
As cute as a button.
As smart as a fox.

As thick as a brick.
As lonely as a worm.
As weak as a kitten.
As filthy as a germ.

**Deni Acres (7)**
**Green Wrythe Primary School**

# She Is . . .

As busy as a bee.
As patient as Job.
As happy as Larry.
As white as a dressing robe.

As cool as a cucumber.
As neat as a pin.
As likely as not.
As ugly as sin.

As straight as an arrow.
As sturdy as an oak.
As pale as death.
As aged as old folk.

As tall as a giraffe.
As clean as a whistle.
As cute as a cupcake.
As Scottish as thistle.

**Jolie Hamilton-Warford  (9)**
**Green Wrythe Primary School**

# Young Writers Information

We hope you have enjoyed reading this book - and that you will continue to enjoy it in the coming years.

If you like reading and writing poetry drop us a line, or give us a call, and we'll send you a free information pack.

Alternatively if you would like to order further copies of this book or any of our other titles, then please give us a call or log onto our website at www.youngwriters.co.uk

**Young Writers Information
Remus House
Coltsfoot Drive
Peterborough
PE2 9JX**

**(01733) 890066**